THE CELTIC COLLECTION

Cover Photo: Beth A. Sablay

ISBN 978-0-634-01222-8

HAL•LEONARD®
CORPORATION

7777 W. BLUEMOUND RD. P.O. BOX 13819 MILWAUKEE, WI 53213

Visit Hal Leonard Online at
www.halleonard.com

CONTENTS

FROM THE ARRANGER...

To my musical friends,

I am writing these arrangements as September draws to a close. The view out my studio window includes rosebushes that are beginning to look a little "tired." For this reason, the lyric to "'Tis the Last Rose of Summer" is particularly stirring to me.

'Tis the last rose of summer left blooming alone.
All her lovely companions are faded and gone.
No flower of her kindred, no rosebud is nigh
To reflect back her blushes or give sigh for sigh.

There is something about an Irish folk song that never fails to charm me. The spacious melodies can be both haunting and heartwarming. The insistent rhythm of a jig creates energy that is undeniably infectious.

In these settings, I have attempted to bring the flavor of the flute, fiddle and bagpipe to the piano. Experiment with the grace notes; placing them on or after the downbeat will provide different, yet equally effective results. The dynamic extremes are essential to bringing the color of these arrangements into full bloom.

With best wishes,
Phillip Keveren

Phillip Keveren, a multi-talented keyboard artist and composer, has composed original works in a variety of genres from piano solo to symphonic orchestra. Mr. Keveren gives frequent concerts and workshops for teachers and their students in the United States, Canada, Europe, and Asia. Mr. Keveren holds a B.M. in composition from California State University Northridge and a M.M. in composition from the University of Southern California.

BE THOU MY VISION

Ancient Irish poem
Translated by MARY E. BYRNE
Traditional Irish melody

Slowly, spaciously

Gently flowing

DANNY BOY
(LONDONDERRY AIR)

Lyric by FREDERICK EDWARD WEATHERLY
Music based on the Irish Folksong, "Londonderry Air"

With melancholy

THE CROPPY BOY

18th Century Irish Folksong

DOWN BY THE SALLEY GARDENS

Lyric by WILLIAM BUTLER YEATS
Music by HERBERT HUGHES

THE GALWAY PIPER

Irish Folksong

GARRYOWEN

18th Century Irish Folksong

THE IRISH WASHERWOMAN

Irish Folksong

THE LARK IN THE CLEAR AIR

Lyric and Music by
SIR SAMUEL FERGUSON

KITTY OF COLERAINE

Lyric by EDWARD LYSAGHT
Music by AILEEN ROWE

LET ERIN REMEMBER THE DAYS OF OLD

Lyric by THOMAS MOORE
Music based on the Irish Folksong, "The Red Fox"

MOLLY MALONE
(COCKLES & MUSSELS)

Irish Folksong

MOLLY BRANNIGAN

Irish Folksong

To Coda ⊕

THE PARTING GLASS

Irish Folksong

Steadily, with motion

With pedal

'TIS THE LAST ROSE OF SUMMER

Lyric by THOMAS MOORE
Music by RICHARD ALFRED MILLIKEN

Slowly, with melancholy

THE WEARING OF THE GREEN

Lyric by DION BOUCICAULT
18th Century Irish Folksong

Be Thou My Vision
(Ancient Irish poem, translated by Mary E. Byrne)

1. Be Thou my vision, O Lord of my heart;
   Naught be all else to me, save that Thou art.
   Thou my best thought, by day or by night;
   Waking or sleeping, Thy presence my light.

2. Riches I heed not, nor vain, empty praise.
   Thou mine inheritance, now and always.
   Thou and Thou only, first in my heart,
   Great God of heaven, my treasure Thou art.

3. Be Thou my wisdom, and Thou my true word;
   I ever with Thee and Thou with me, Lord.
   Heart of my own heart, whatever befall,
   Still be my vision, O Ruler of all.

4. High King of heaven, when victory is won,
   May I reach heaven's joys, bright heaven's sun!
   Heart of my heart, whatever befall,
   Still be my vision, O Ruler of all.

The Croppy Boy

1. 'Twas early, early in the spring;
   The birds did whistle and sweetly sing,
   Changing their notes from tree to tree,
   And the song they sang was "Old Ireland Free."

2. 'Twas early, early in the night;
   The yeoman cavalry gave me a fright.
   The yeoman cavalry was my downfall,
   And taken was I by the Lord Cornwall.

3. 'Twas in the guardhouse where I was laid,
   And in the parlor where I was tried.
   My sentence passed and my courage low,
   When to Dungannon I was forced to go.

4. As I was passing my father's door,
   My brother William stood at the door.
   My aged father stood there also;
   My tender mother, her hair she tore.

5. As I was going up Wexford Hill,
   Who could blame me to cry my fill?
   I looked behind and I looked before;
   My aged mother I shall see no more.

6. As I was mounted on the scaffold high,
   My aged father was standing by.
   My aged father did me deny,
   And the name he gave me was the Croppy Boy.

7. 'Twas in the Dungannon this young man died,
   And in Dungannon his body lies.
   And you good people that do pass by,
   Oh, shed a tear for the Croppy Boy.

Danny Boy
(Londonderry Air)
(Lyric by Frederick Edward Weatherly)

1. Oh, Danny Boy, the pipes, the pipes are calling
   From glen to glen and down the mountainside.
   The summer's gone, and all the roses falling;
   It's you, it's you must go and I must bide.
   But come ye back when summer's in the meadow,
   Or when the valley's hush'd and white with snow;
   'Tis I'll be there in sunshine or in shadow.
   Oh, Danny Boy, oh Danny Boy, I love you so!

2. But if he come, when all the flow'rs are dying,
   And I am dead, as dead I well may be,
   Ye'll come and find the place where I am lying,
   And kneel and say an *Ave* there for me.
   And I shall hear, tho' soft your tread above me,
   And all my dreams will warm and sweeter be.
   If you will not fail to tell me that you love me,
   Then I shall sleep in peace until you come to me!

Down by the Salley Gardens

(Lyric by William Butler Yeats)

1. Down by the salley gardens my love and I did meet.
   She passed the salley gardens with little snow-white feet.
   She bid me take love easy, as the leaves grow on the tree.
   But I, being young and foolish, with her did not agree.

2. In a field by the river my love and I did stand,
   And leaning on my shoulder she laid her snow-white hand.
   She bid me take life easy, as the grass grows on the weirs.
   But I was young and foolish, and now am full of tears.

The Galway Piper

1. Ev'ry person in the nation
   Or of great or humble station
   Holds in highest estimation
   Piping Tim of Galway.
   Loudly he can play, or low;
   He can move you, fast or slow.
   Touch your hearts or stir your toe,
   Piping Tim of Galway.

2. When the wedding bells are ringing,
   His the breath that stirs the singing.
   Then in jigs the folks go swinging.
   What a splendid piper!
   He will blow from eve to morn,
   Counting sleep a thing of scorn.
   Old is he, but not out-worn.
   Know you such a piper?

3. When he walks the highway pealing,
   'Round his head the birds come wheeling.
   Tim has carols worth the stealing,
   Piping Tim of Galway.
   Thrush and linnet, finch and lark
   To each other twitter, "Hark!"
   Soon they sing from light to dark
   Pipings learnt in Galway.

Garryowen

1. Let Bacchus' sons be not dismayed,
   But join with me each jovial blade.
   Come booze and sing and lend your aid
   To help me with the chorus.

   Chorus:
   Instead of spa we'll drink down ale
   And pay the reck'ning on the nail.
   No man for debt shall go to jail
   From Garryowen in glory.

2. We are the boys that take delight
   In smashing the limerick lights when lighting.
   Through all the streets like sporters fighting
   And tearing all before us. *(To chorus:)*

3. We'll break the windows, we'll break the doors,
   The watch knock down by threes and fours.
   Then let the doctors work their cures
   And tinker up our bruises. *(To chorus:)*

4. We'll beat the bailiffs out of fun,
   We'll make the mayors and sheriffs run.
   We are the boys no man dares dun
   If he regards a whole skin. *(To chorus:)*

5. Our hearts so stout have got us fame,
   For soon 'tis known from whence we came.
   Where'er we go they dread the name
   Of Garryowen in glory. *(To chorus:)*

Kitty of Coleraine

(Lyric by Edward Lysaght)

1. As beautiful Kitty one morning was tripping
   With a pitcher of milk from the fair of Coleraine,
   When she saw me, she stumbled. The pitcher, it tumbled,
   And all the sweet buttermilk watered the plain.
   "Oh, what shall I do now? 'Twas looking at you, now!
   Sure, sure, such a pitcher I'll ne'er meet again.
   'Twas the pride of my dairy. Oh, Barney McCleary,
   You're sent as a plague to the girls of Coleraine!"

2. I sat down beside her and gently did chide her
   That such a misfortune should give her such pain.
   A kiss then I gave her, and before I did leave her
   She vowed for such pleasure she'd break it again.
   'Twas haymaking season, I can't tell the reason,
   Misfortune will never come single, 'tis plain,
   For very soon after poor Kitty's disaster
   There was not a pitcher found whole in Coleraine.

The Lark in the Clear Air
(Lyric by Sir Samuel Ferguson)

1. Dear thoughts are in my mind,
   And my soul soars enchanted,
   As I hear the sweet lark sing
   In the clear air of the day.
   For a tender, beaming smile
   To my hope has been granted,
   And tomorrow she shall hear
   All my fond heart would say.

2. I shall tell her all my love,
   All my soul's adoration,
   And I think she will hear me,
   And will not say me nay.
   It is this that gives my soul
   All its joyous elation,
   As I hear the sweet lark sing
   In the clear air of the day.

Let Erin Remember the Days of Old
(Lyric by Thomas Moore)

1. Let Erin remember the days of old,
   Ere her faithless sons betray'd her;
   When Malachi wore the collar of gold,
   Which he won from her proud invader;
   When her kings with standards of green unfurl'd
   Led the Red-Branch Knights to danger;
   Ere the emerald gem of the western world
   Was set in the crown of a stranger.

2. On Lough Neagh's bank as the fisherman strays,
   When the clear, cold eve's declining,
   He sees the round towers of other days
   In the wave beneath him shining!
   Thus shall memory often, in dreams sublime,
   Catch a glimpse of the days that are over;
   Thus, sighing, look through the waves of time
   For the long faded glories they cover!

Molly Brannigan

1. Ma'am dear, did ye never hear of pretty Molly Brannigan?
   In throth, then, she's left me, and I'll never be a man again.
   Not a spot on my hide will a summer's sun e'er tan again,
   Since Molly's gone and left me here alone for to die.
   The place where my heart was you'd aisy rowl a turnip in;
   'Tis as large as all Dublin, and from Dublin to the Divil's Glen.
   If she wish'd to take another, sure she might have left mine back again,
   And not have gone and left me here alone for to die.

2. Ma'am dear, I remember when the milking time was past and gone.
   We strolled thro' the meadow, and she swore I was the only one
   That ever she could love, but oh, the base and cruel one.
   For all that she's left me here alone for to die.
   Ma'am dear, I remember when coming home the rain began,
   I wrapt my friezecoat 'round her and ne'er a waistcoat had I on,
   And my shirt was rather fine drawn, but oh, the false and cruel one.
   For all that she's left me here alone for to die.

3. The left side of my carcass is as weak as water gruel, ma'am.
   There's not a pick upon my bones, since Molly's proved so cruel, ma'am.
   Oh, if I had a blunder gun, I'd go and fight a duel, ma'am.
   For sure I'd better shoot myself than live here to die.
   I'm cool an' determined as any salamander, ma'am.
   Won't you come to my wake when I go the long meander, ma'am?
   I'll think myself as valiant as the famous Alexander, ma'am,
   When I hear ye cryin' o'er me, "Arrah! Why did ye die?"

Molly Malone
(Cockles & Mussels)

1. In Dublin's fair city, where girls are so pretty,
   I first set my eyes on sweet Molly Malone,
   As she pushed her wheelbarrow thro' streets broad and narrow,
   Crying, "Cockles and mussels, alive, alive, oh!
   Alive, alive, oh! Alive, alive, oh!"
   Crying, "Cockles and mussels, alive, alive, oh!"

2. She was a fishmonger, but sure 'twas no wonder,
   For so were her father and mother before.
   And they each wheeled their barrow thro' streets broad and narrow,
   Crying, "Cockles and mussels, alive, alive, oh!
   Alive, alive, oh! Alive, alive, oh!"
   Crying, "Cockles and mussels, alive, alive, oh!"

3. She died of a fever, and no one could save her,
   And that was the end of sweet Molly Malone.
   But her ghost wheels her barrow thro' streets broad and narrow,
   Crying, "Cockles and mussels, alive, alive, oh!
   Alive, alive, oh! Alive, alive, oh!"
   Crying, "Cockles and mussels, alive, alive, oh!"

The Parting Glass

1. O, all the money e'er I had,
   I spent it in good company,
   And all the harm I've ever done,
   Alas! It was to none but me.
   And all I've done for want of wit
   To memory now I can't recall.
   So fill to me the parting glass;
   Goodnight and joy be with you all.

2. O, all the comrades e'er I had,
   They're sorry for my going away.
   And all the sweethearts e'er I had,
   They'd wish me one more day to stay.
   But since it falls unto my lot,
   I gently rise and softly call,
   That I should go and you should not.
   Goodnight and joy be with you all.

3. If I had money enough to spend,
   And leisure time to sit awhile,
   There is a fair maid in this town
   That sorely has my heart beguiled.
   Her rosy cheeks and ruby lips,
   I own she has my heart in thrall.
   Then fill to me the parting glass;
   Goodnight and joy be with you all.

'Tis the Last Rose of Summer

(Lyric by Thomas Moore)

1. 'Tis the last rose of summer left blooming alone.
   All her lovely companions are faded and gone.
   No flower of her kindred, no rosebud is nigh
   To reflect back her blushes or give sigh for sigh.

2. I'll leave thee, thou lone one, to pine on a stem.
   Since the lovely are sleeping, go sleep thou with them.
   Thus, kindly I scatter thy leaves o'er the bed
   Where thy mates of the garden lie scentless and dead.

3. So soon may I follow, when friendships decay
   And from love's shining circle the gems drop away.
   When true hearts lie withered and fond ones are flown,
   Oh, who would inhabit this bleak world alone?

The Wearing of the Green

(Lyric by Dion Boucicault)

1. Oh, Paddy dear, and did you hear the news that's going 'round?
   The shamrock is forbid by law to grow on Irish ground.
   Saint Patrick's Day no more to keep, his color can't be seen,
   For there's a bloody law agin' the wearing of the green.
   I met with Napper Tandy and he took me by the hand,
   And he said, "How's poor old Ireland and how does she stand?"
   "She's the most distressful country that ever you have seen.
   They're hanging men and women there for wearing of the green."

2. Then since the color we must wear is England's cruel red,
   Sure Ireland's sons will ne'er forget the blood that they have shed.
   You may take the shamrock from your hat and cast it on the sod,
   But 'twill take root and flourish still, though under foot it's trod.
   When the law can stop the blades of grass from growing as they grow,
   And when the leaves in summertime their verdure dare not show,
   Then I will change the color that I wear in my corbeen.
   But till that day, please God, I'll stick to wearing of the green!

3. But, if at last our color should be torn from Ireland's heart,
   Her sons, with shame and sorrow, from the dear old soil will part.
   I've heard whispers of a country that lies far beyond the sea,
   Where rich and poor stand equal in the light of freedom's day.
   Oh, Erin, must we leave you, driven by the tyrant's hand?
   Must we ask a mother's welcome from a strange, but happier land?
   Where the cruel cross of England's thraldom never shall be seen,
   And where, thank God, we'll live and die still wearing of the green.